HEALING
RELATIONSHIPS
THROUGH FORGIVENESS

*EXPERIENCING GOD'S GRACE FOR
OURSELVES*

A WORKBOOK COMPANION
FOR GROUP STUDY
PART 1

DONALD E. JONES, PHD

J & A BOOK PUBLISHERS
www.jabookpublishers.com

ISBN-13: 978-0692741177
ISBN-10: 0692741178

DEDICATION

I dedicate this book to my Savior and Lord Jesus Christ. He has been with me every step of my journey upon the earth, and I so look forward to being in His presence forever and ever.

CONTENTS

ACKNOWLEDGMENTS

I want to thank my wonderful and gracious wife Carol who has supported me in this ministry with sacrifice, enthusiasm, encouragement, and accountability. Most of all, she has been a constant blessing because of her willingness to listen. I was always sharing with her the truths God had been teaching me as I studied His word and wrote this book. It consumed many hours. Thank you, Carol, and I deeply love you.

I want to thank my son Gregory R. Jones for volunteering to be the primary editor of this important book. Without his time and effort in painstakingly and meticulously going over every word and every sentence checking and rechecking the sentence structure and grammar, I would not have been able to complete it. Thank you for your ministry to me. I love you my son.

I want to thank my other children, Krista, Matt, and Kara for their love for Christ and His Word and their willingness to live for Him. I love you all.

Introduction

This workbook is designed to aid in the comprehension and application of the truths from the Scriptures which are found in the book of the same name. It has a question and answer format because asking questions was a powerful teaching method that the Lord used to reveal God's divine truth. Jesus asked over one hundred and thirty questions as He instructed the people of God and others. These are only the recorded ones. We can only speculate as to how many questions He might have actually asked. The Lord used His questioning techniques to prompt His listeners to focus, understand, analyze, evaluate, and apply the principles He was proclaiming to them. The same has been done in this workbook.

In Mark chapter 2, Jesus enters Capernaum after a long absence. His reputation for performing great miracles had increased. His arrival caused an instant reaction, and many rushed to the home where He was residing. They desired for them or a loved one to be healed. Among the crowd were a group of Pharisees (a sect of legalistic Jews) and Scribes (a group of Jewish theologians) who had also hurried to see how they could trap Him in something He said or did. To hide their presence, they mingled among the massive crowd. It was a large town with a large crowd gathered in a small home.

Jesus was probably standing in the open courtyard which was in the center of the home surrounded by various rooms. The door or gate to the courtyard was blocked by the people. Four men brought a paralyzed man to see if Jesus would heal him. They could not enter the home due to the crowd and decided to enter another less obvious way. The roofs in ancient times were made of several beams, thick mud, and straw. The stairs to the roof were on the outside of the home attached to the side. So, these four men carried the paralyzed man on a mat up to the roof. There they began digging out a portion of the roof to drop the man into the courtyard. As the Lord was teaching, this man was being lowered down right in front of Him.

The Messiah marveled at their faith and addressed the paralyzed man. In verse 5, Mark records, "Jesus, seeing their faith, said to the paralytic, "Son, your sins are forgiven you." Though not mentioned, Jesus would have peered into the man's heart and seen his repentance and the belief in Him as Savior and Lord. Here, Jesus is demonstrating that He is God because only God can forgive sins. The Pharisees and Scribes must have gasped and thought, "Who does this man think he is? Only God can forgive sins.

As these men were pondering this, the Lord Jesus looked at them and asked a piercing question. In verse 8-9, Mark describes it in these words, "Immediately Jesus, perceiving in his spirit that they so reasoned within themselves, said to them, 'Why do you reason these things in your hearts? Which is easier, to tell the paralytic, 'Your sins are forgiven;' or to say, 'Arise, and take up your bed, and walk?'" This question forced them to the heart of the matter. Anyone could claim to forgive sins, but He was able prove it by an astounding miracle only God could do. He could make the man walk. So, Jesus commanded the man to take up his pallet and walk. Then, Son of God declared that he had demonstrated that He did have the divine power to forgive sins as He had the divine power to heal. Well, the crowd was utterly astonished and began to glorify God. As Jesus used questions, so shall we. May the questions in this book help you focus, understand, analyze, evaluate, and apply these biblical principles.

Chapter 1

Involve God First

The first important step in the reconciliation process is the recognition that no matter who else we have sinned against, we have sinned against our God first.

In the section, "A Typical Scenario," the author describes an argument someone might have had with another that could require a reconciliation.

What is the scenario about?

What did the conflict concern?

What was the relationship between the parties?

Have you had a similar experience?

In the section, "A Scriptural Principle" the author presents an important biblical principle in the forgiveness process which concerns our sins against God in relationships.

How would you express this principle in your own words?

How would you rewrite this principle to make it even more personal to your life (using your name and situation)?

Why do you think this principle might be important in your life right now?

How would you rate yourself on the percentage of times you followed this principle in the past when you did something wrong in a relationship?

Directions: Put a horizontal mark and your name where you see yourself on the percentage line.

0%	25%	50%	75%	100%

In the section, "A Biblical Explanation," the author explains the reasons why our sin is first against the Lord God when we sin against others in a relationship and what we should do about it.

In Psalm 51:4, what did King David really mean when he wrote "against you and you alone" have I sinned?

Why must the Lord God be dealt with on an "utterly divine level" when we transgress others?

According to Psalm 41:4 and 11–13, what will we experience when we confess our sins to God first?

According to Matthew 6:12 (the Lord's Prayer), what must we do before we forgive others?

According to Psalm 86:5, when we come to God and ask for forgiveness what is He ready to do?

In what ways might these truths impact your relationships?

In the section, "An Ancient Portrait," the author provides the unique portrayal of King David's sin with Bathsheba and its resultant cover-up.

What was David's sin against Uriah?

How did David attempt to cover up his sin?

How did God feel about what David had done?

What was David's response after Nathan confronted him?

Though not mentioned, what would David have needed to do once he had reconciled with God?

Have you ever been in any situation comparable to David's who attempted to cover up his sin or Uriah's who had somebody try and deceive him? How was it different and how was it the same?

In the section, "A Modern Anecdote," the author discusses a situation in which a woman's alcohol consumption reached an extreme level and the problems that occurred.

How had the wife's drinking problem escalate to the point that she needed counseling for her and her husband?

What individual responsibility did the wife and her husband bear for her difficulties with alcohol?

How did the both of them improperly handle the drinking problem?

What are two biblical reasons (with verses) why this was not the best approach?

How did the couple begin the reconciliation process using the Scriptural principle discussed in this chapter?

Based on the truths learned in this chapter, what would you have done differently if you were the wife or the husband?

In the section, "A Personal Response," the author provides a model you may use for prayer if you find it necessary after discovering the truths in this chapter.

Are you presently in a relationship where you have sinned against another and have not asked God for forgiveness? If not, is there one from the past that still needs this prayer to be prayed?

Based on the truths you have just learned, what will you continue doing in your current relationships and what will you do differently?

What additional thoughts would you like to share with the others?

Chapter 2

Leave Nothing Out

As we ask for forgiveness, we must realize God knows every detail of what we have done. So, we must confess all our wrong-doing in the relationship and hold nothing back.

In the section, "A Typical Scenario," the author describes an encounter one might have with a customer representative on the phone which may require a reconciliation.

What is the scenario about?

What did the conflict concern?

What was the relationship between the parties?

Have you had a similar experience?

In the section, "A Scriptural Principle" the author presents an important biblical principle in the forgiveness process which concerns our sin against God.

How would you express this principle in your own words?

How would you rewrite this principle to make it even more personal to your life (using your name and situation)?

Why do you think this principle might be important in your life right now?

How would you rate yourself on the percentage of times you followed this principle in the past when you did something wrong in a relationship?

Directions: Put a horizontal mark and your name where you are on the percentage line.

_____

0%   25%   50%   75%   100%

In the section, "A Biblical Explanation," the author explains the reasons why we should to own up to all our sins against others in a relationship and what we should do about it.

According to David's words in Psalm 32:3-4, and 11, what did he feel before and then after he confessed all his sins?

What are two examples (with the passages that support them) of individuals who acknowledged that God's people should confess all of their sins before Him?

In 1 Kings 8:50, what key phrase is used to indicate that Solomon was asking God to forgive every sin of His people?

In Psalm 90:8, what key phrase is used to indicate that Moses was asking God to forgive all the sins of His people?

According to Psalm 139:4 and Hebrews 4:12, how might we discover the sins we have committed in a relationship?

In what ways might these truths impact your relationships?

In the section, "An Ancient Portrait," the author provides an example of Adam and Eve committing a sin against God and their unwillingness to own up to all that they did.

When God placed Adam and Eve in the garden, what were they to do?

What was the transgression that Adam and Eve committed which destroyed their initial relationship to God?

Rather than admit all he had done, who did Adam blame?

Rather than admit all she had done, who did Eve blame?

Did God give them opportunities to admit all they had done wrong to Him?

Have you ever been in a situation that was similar to Adam and Eve's in which you or the other person blamed someone else for wrong-doing? How was it different and how was it the same?

In the section, "A Modern Anecdote," the author discusses a situation in which a husband had to own up to all the sins he committed in his sinful pornography habit before God.

How did the husband's pornography obsession negatively impact his relationship to his wife?

How did the husband feel after his wife found out?

What initial steps did the husband have to take to reconcile his relationship with God and then his wife?

Did this process come easily for the couple?

Did the wife desire to accept any responsibility for what her husband had done? Should she have? Why or why not?

Based on the truths learned in this chapter, what would you have done differently if you were husband or wife?

In the section, "A Personal Response," the author provides a model you may use for prayer if you find it necessary after discovering the truths in this chapter.

Are you presently in a relationship where you have sinned against another and have not asked God for forgiveness? If not, is there one from the past that still needs this prayer to be prayed?

Based on the truths you have just learned, what will you continue doing in your current relationships and what will you do differently?

What additional thoughts would you like to share with the others?

Chapter 3

Admit Your Sin

To restore our relationship with God, He desires us to confess our sins before Him. This is a three-fold process as we admit our sins, mourn over them, and turn from them.

In the section, "A Typical Scenario," the author describes an encounter one might have with a police officer that did not go well and may require a reconciliation.

What is the scenario about?

What did the conflict concern?

What was the relationship between the parties?

Have you had a similar experience?

In the section, "A Scriptural Principle" the author presents an important biblical principle in the forgiveness process which concerns the confession of our sins against God.

How would you express this principle in your own words?

How would you rewrite this principle to make it even more personal to your life (using your name and situation)?

Why do you think this principle might be important in your life right now?

How would you rate yourself on the percentage of times you followed this principle in the past when you did something wrong in a relationship?

Directions: Put a horizontal mark and your name where you are on the percentage line.

0%	25%	50%	75%	100%

In the section, "A Biblical Explanation," the author explains the reasons why we are to fully confess all the sins against others in a relationship and how to do it.

According to 1 John 1:8, what can we never say about sin in general or in our relationships?

According to 1 John 1:9, once we realize we have sinned in a relationship what should we do?

What it the first characteristic of a repentant heart (provide a verse)?

What it the second characteristic of a truly repentant heart (provide a verse)?

What it the third characteristic of a repentant heart (provide a verse)?

In what ways might these truths impact your relationships?

In the section, "An Ancient Portrait," the author provides a devastating situation for Israel when Achan was unwilling to confess his sin before God.

What was Achan's sin against Israel?

How did Achan cover it up?

What did Joshua want Achan to do before he received his just punishment?

What qualities of repentance did Achan not demonstrate?

What was Achan's punishment and why was God so harsh?

Have you ever been in a situation comparable to Israel's in which others did not own up to their sins against you or like Achan's in which you did not take any responsibility against them? How was it different and how was it the same?

In the section, "A Modern Anecdote," the author describes an encounter with a young man who was not able to leave the home when he became an adult.

What difficulties did the mother and father have with each other that led to their son being unable to leave the home?

How was his joy with his parents much different than his joy with his friends? Why?

What unhealthy behaviors did the young man engage in to cope with the struggles of his parents?

What individual responsibility should the son have taken for his own failure to leave the home?

How did the parents and the son reconcile with each other in order for the young man to leave the home?

Based on the truths learned in this chapter, what would you have done differently if you were one of the parents or the young man?

In the section, "A Personal Response," the author provides a model you may use for prayer if you find it necessary after discovering the truths in this chapter.

Are you presently in a relationship where you have sinned against another and have not asked God for forgiveness? If not, is there one from the past that still needs this prayer to be prayed?

Based on the truths you have just learned, what will you continue doing in your current relationships and what will you do differently?

What additional thoughts would you like to share with the others?

Chapter 4

Accept God's Forgiveness

The next step is to accept God's forgiveness with a sense of blessing and gratefulness. Any sin or transgression that we could commit has already been forgiven.

In the section, "A Typical Scenario," the author describes an unpleasant dream in which one may suddenly realize all the sins he or she has committed, especially in relationships.

What is the scenario about?

What did the conflict concern?

What was the relationship between the parties?

Have you had a similar experience?

In the section, "A Scriptural Principle" the author presents an important biblical principle in the forgiveness process which concerns fully accepting God's forgiveness.

How would you express this principle in your own words?

How would you rewrite this principle to make it even more personal to your life (using your name and situation)?

Why do you think this principle might be important in your life right now?

How would you rate yourself on the percentage of times you followed this principle in the past when you did something wrong in a relationship?

Directions: Put a horizontal mark and your name where you are on the percentage line.

0%	25%	50%	75%	100%

In the section, "A Biblical Explanation," the author explains the reasons for accepting the forgiveness of God for our sins against others with a sense of blessing and gratefulness and how to do it.

According to Colossians 2:13-14, what has happened to the past sins we have committed in our relationships?

According to Hebrews 9:22, what sacrifice had to be made for our forgiveness of sins that we commit in relationships?

According to Romans 4:8 and Psalm 28:7, how should we feel about God's forgiveness of our relationship sins?

According to Hebrews 10:22, how does forgiveness compare to washing with pure water?

Does God have enough grace to forgive these sins no matter how great? How do you know (provide verse)?

In what ways might these truths impact your relationships?

In the section, "An Ancient Portrait," the author provides a picture of a woman who entered Simon's home to see Jesus. The woman repented and accepted His forgiveness with a sense of blessing and gratitude.

According to Simon, what kind of person was the woman?

Why didn't Simon understand what the woman was doing?

What three actions did the woman take to demonstrate her repentance?

What was the Lord's gracious response?

How did Simon dishonor Jesus in what he did not do?

Have you ever been in a situation similar to the woman's in which you sought forgiveness or Simon's where you may have been critical? How was it different and how was it the same?

In the section, "A Modern Anecdote," the author shares the good news with a woman who could not believe the Lord God would forgive all her sins.

What happened in the woman's life that made her feel so empty inside?

Why did the author share the gospel with her?

What does God, the Father, provide people with when they become Christians?

What held the woman back from receiving Jesus Christ as Savior and Lord?

What should the woman do if she makes more mistakes?

Based on the truths learned in this chapter, did you react in the same kind of way when you became a Christian or have you since felt this way when you sinned against another?

In the section, "A Personal Response," the author provides a model you may use for prayer if you find it necessary after discovering the truths in this chapter.

Are you presently in a relationship where you have sinned against another and have not asked God for forgiveness? If not, is there one from the past that still needs this prayer to be prayed?

Based on the truths you have just learned, what will you continue doing in your current relationships and what will you do differently?

What additional thoughts would you like to share with the others?

Chapter 5

Forgive Yourself All

Now, we must fully forgive ourselves. Though this may be difficult at times, God does not desire His children to feel guilty for their sins after confessing them.

In the section, "A Typical Scenario," the author describes an encounter with someone who had not forgiven himself for a sin he had committed in a relationship.

What is the scenario about?

What did the conflict concern?

What was the relationship between the parties?

Have you had a similar experience?

In the section, "A Scriptural Principle" the author presents an important biblical principle in the forgiveness process which concerns forgiving ourselves.

How would you express this principle in your own words?

How would you rewrite this principle to make it even more personal to your life (using your name and situation)?

Why do you think this principle might be important in your life right now?

How would you rate yourself on the percentage of times you followed this principle in the past when you did something wrong in a relationship?

Directions: Put a horizontal mark and your name where you are on the percentage line.

| 0% | 25% | 50% | 75% | 100% |

In the section, "A Biblical Explanation," the author explains the reasons why we are to forgive ourselves for the sins we commit against others in a relationship and how to do it.

According to Romans 7:20, what is inside us which keeps us from forgiving ourselves?

According to 2 Corinthians 10:5, what must we do with the false concept that our sin is too great or sins too numerous for us to forgive ourselves?

According to Romans 12:2, how can we subdue these guilt-filled thoughts that condemn?

According to Philippians 4:6–7, what must we do to guard our hearts and minds from these unforgiving thoughts?

When a memory of a sin against another returns, how are we to handle it?

In what ways might these truths impact your relationships?

In the section, "An Ancient Portrait," the author describes how Peter handled his grievous sin against the Lord and the guilt which must have accompanied it.

What was Peter's attitude when Jesus told him that he would deny him three times that night?

How did Peter actually deny Christ?

What was Peter's response after he had denied Christ?

What were the consequences of Peter's denial?

Why do you think Peter was silent about his sin in his letters (1 and 2 Peter)?

Have you ever been in a situation like Peter's in which you knew God forgave your sin against another, but you could not forgive yourself? How was it different and how was it the same?

In the section, "A Modern Anecdote," the author describes a deep struggle a husband had to forgive himself for the sin of adultery.

What did the husband mean when he said "I am that guy?"

What does a healthy fear in a relationship involve?

Why was the husband filled with anxiety?

According to Romans 7:20, where did the condemning voice inside his head come from?

What might be some safeguards the family could set up to rebuild the trust and keep this sin from occurring again?

Based on the truths learned in this chapter, how would you have reacted to your sin if you were the husband? How would you have acted if you were the wife?

In the section, "A Personal Response," the author provides a model you may use for prayer if you find it necessary after discovering the truths in this chapter.

Are you presently in a relationship where you have sinned against another and have not asked God for forgiveness? If not, is there one from the past that still needs this prayer to be prayed?

Based on the truths you have just learned, what will you continue doing in your current relationships and what will you do differently?

What additional thoughts would you like to share with the others?

Conclusion

As we conclude this book, I would like to leave us with some final thoughts about our God of forgiveness and what His Son did on the cross for us. First, if we understand the full extent of what was wrought for us on that cursed tree in order to forgive us, it will become so much easier to do the same thing for others. Second, if you read this entire book and realized that you do not understand salvation or have never received Christ as Lord and Savior, then I would like to provide that opportunity. Please do not skip this section; it may be the most important in your life.

From all outward appearances, humans seem "good" and attempt to live decent lives. This is man's concept of himself. This is not God's concept. The Almighty's view is that people all over the world and throughout the ages sin, sin, and sin again (Romans 3:23). This is a terrible and utterly destructive condition. Yet, they have ramifications that are far worse. These sins condemn us to everlasting divine retribution.

Though described briefly in the Old Testament, the Lord Jesus Christ clearly announced and proclaimed the future punishment to come. Contrary to popular belief, Jesus did not only speak of love, grace, and mercy, He also spoke of the coming judgment for sin. He declared that the judgment of sin would be everlasting punishment in a place He called "Hell." The Lord portrayed this place as an eternal inferno (Matthew 18:8) where there would be the weeping (from the sorrow) and gnashing of teeth (from the agony and anguish of suffering) continually into eternity (Matthew 8:12; 13:42, 50; 22:13; 24:51; 25:30; Luke 13:28).

Why must people face this horrific punishment? Though God is a God of love, grace, and mercy, He is also a God of great holiness, righteousness, and justice (Psalm 89:14,18). These attributes are just as much a part of His divine nature as His love, grace, and mercy. You have broken God's law as we all have and the penalty must be paid. This began with the first man Adam (Genesis 3:1-7). When this occurred, His love, grace, and mercy surfaced and a provision was made. Someone else would have to take man's place and pay the penalty. Someone who had never transgressed Him, who would never deserve punishment, and would fulfill all of God's Laws, would be substituted in man's place. This was the Son of God, Jesus Christ.

As the God-Man, He would pay the penalty for our sins in His death on the cross. Once done, the Lord God made only one provision for people to appropriate what His Son had done on the cross for them. This provision is receiving Jesus Christ as Savior and Lord. Though I cannot possibly share with you this good news in the confines of this book, I would love for you to consider purchasing my book entitled, *Finding The Light: The Kingdom of Heaven and How To Enter It.* It can be found for sale on Amazon.com. It is inexpensive and contains the full gospel message for your consideration. This message is so important and extensive that it cannot adequately be contained in a few pages at the end of a book.

If you are a believer, you must go out into the world and forgive as you are forgiven. These principles are to be lived and shared with others. You now have the tools to make your relationships last a lifetime. Go live them out and share them with others!

ABOUT THE AUTHOR

Dr. Donald Jones is currently a Christian Pastoral Counselor with thirty-eight years of experience in the fields of pastoral ministry, public education, and Christian counseling. He carries degrees and certificates from four major universities and from a variety of educational institutions. He has been a professor of Languages and Bible, a television commentator, and a featured speaker at a variety of events and seminars at churches, schools, and other organizations across the United States. He is a member in good standing of several secular and Christian professional organizations. Dr. Jones has been a published author since 1976. For further information view his website at www.donjonesphd.com.

www.ingramcontent.com/pod-product-compliance
Lightning Source LLC
Chambersburg PA
CBHW030309030426
42337CB00012B/652